Words of Wisdom
Words of Faith

Inspiration & Motivation from a 97 Year Old!

How To Pray, Develop Strong Belief & Faith, and Live Life on Your Terms!

Hyacinth Mottley

Copyright © 2012 – Hyacinth Mottley and Marcus Mottley

All rights reserved. No part of this publication may be reproduced, distributed, or transmitted in any form or by any means, including photocopying, recording, or other electronic or mechanical methods, without the prior written permission of the publisher, except in the case of brief quotations embodied in critical reviews and certain other noncommercial uses permitted by copyright law. For permission, requests, write to the publisher at the address below.

Life Management Publishing
4401-A Connecticut Ave. NW #281
Washington, DC 20011
mpowerme@SpeakTrain.com
www.Speak-Train.com
www.SpeakTrain.com

Printed in the United States of America

Table of Contents

Acknowledgements 4
Preface 6
Introduction 8
    My Childhood Days 11
    Coming to Antigua 15
My Prayers 18
    Why I Pray 19
    Other Selected Thoughts on Prayer 22
    My Personal Prayer of Protection 28
    A Prayer of Reverence 30
    Prayer for Success 32
    Prayer for Formidable Assistance 33
    More About Praying 34
    Pray With Your Legs 36
My Life in Antigua 38
Working in Antigua 39
    1950 Hurricane 43
    Starting My Own Business 44
    My Specialty 46
Words & Thoughts To My Son 50
Health 57

    Physic Nut 59
    Turkey Berry Tree 61
Social Life & Politics 62
    Relationships: Respect Yourself 63
    Friendships 65
    Poverty 67
    Thoughts on Money 69
    Debt 72
    Tithing 75
    Family 76
    Selected Thoughts on Politics & Social Life 78
On Parenting 86
    Home is the Training School for Abroad 91
Thoughts on Faith & Wisdom 94
    Hard Work 95
    Teaching 97
    Avoid Business Partnerships 99
    Control Your Own Thoughts 100
    The Power of Belief 103
    Believe in Yourself – Not in What People Say 106
    Live Life to the Fullest 108
    Other Thoughts and Perspectives 109
What Lies Ahead? 115

Acknowledgements

I have had a long and full life and because of this there is a long list of persons who supported me and to whom I am very grateful. The list is too long to mention everyone. The extraordinary thing is that many of these individuals have passed away, yet my memory of them and the tangible results of their assistance live on through me, my son and my grandsons.

I would like to thank Nurse Avon Tonge for her enduring help over the last fifteen years. Cicely Gomes and Cynthia Williams have been especially helpful – the relationship with them has been more one of family than of friendship. I would also like to thank Keithroy Davis for his kind support over the years.

Mrs. Sarah Athill and her family have embraced me as their own, making me an integral part of the family. When a hurricane devastated my home in 1995, the Athills were there for me. I thank them from the bottom of my heart. Cleon has a very special place in my heart. She is not only the mother of my grandsons. She is not only my son's loving partner. To me she is like a daughter to whom I turn and whom I trust.

I have lived my life for my son, Marcus. He has been a good and loving son and a rock that I can now lean on.

To my grandsons, Tijani and Yohance: The world is before you. Use your time, energy, knowledge, skills and money wisely. 'Be penny wise and pound wise'. Set yourself on a course of learning advanced knowledge and gaining high skills. Stay on course even in the midst of temptations and difficulties that may lie ahead. Captain your own ship and control your own destiny. Be the masters of your world.

To you the reader: Thanks for taking the time to read my story and my thoughts. Thanks for purchasing my book!

Hyacinth Mottley
January, 2012

Preface

Many of the words and thoughts in this book are extracted from letters that I sent to my son after he left Antigua to go to the United States to study. He was accepted at the Maharishi International University and attended the campus in Washington, D.C.

I was very surprised to find out that he has kept letters that I wrote beginning in 1984. Reading these letters brings tears to my eyes and gladness to my heart. These letters and the words in them provide me with solid evidence that prayer works and that family is forever.

Over the past few years, in the writing of this book, I have added to and refined many of the thoughts expressed in those letters. Many of my ideas might challenge the casual reader but I am confident that those who read more deeply will be inspired.

The process of writing this has dug up hurts, passions, loves and blessings… and it has been a good experience. When I thought that my memory would have betrayed me regarding long ago events – it has not. I remember many things from childhood, that even now, bring a kind of mystical smile to my heart.

I have got to say this… I can't believe that 97 years have passed so quickly. Where did the time go? That, I hope should be a lesson to all readers… time will pass. What are you doing with the years in between?

My son once read a poem to me entitled "The Dash" by Linda Ellis. It is a beautiful poem. It references someone who lived a long life and noted the date when they were born and the date when they died. It asks the question about what the little dash between the years meant. What had the person done in those years? In my case, I was born May 13, 1914. I am still here, so my dash is still open: 1914 – ? This book is about that little dash!

I hope that you are using your <u>dash</u> wisely.

May your years be as strengthening to you as my years have been fortifying for me.

Introduction

My Background

My name is Hyacinth Mottley. I was born on the island of Barbados. My mother Eldica Daisley Mottley died when I was four years old. I had one brother who was four years older than me.

My father was from the village called Spooners Hill, in an area called Long Gap which is in the parish of St. Michael. After my mother's death, my brother and I were taken to the countryside to live with my uncle's wife, Ms. Eloise Mottley, who became my adopted mother.

My adopted mother had two children of her own – a girl and a boy. The girl, Eudora Felicia Mottley, migrated to the United States and became a violin professor. This proved to me that we can be anything we want to be … providing that we want to be something! However, we must set your goals and keep stepping. The road may not be always smooth or straight. But when you have an ambition, focus your attention on what you really want and success will come after you have travelled around the bends and up and down the hills, across ponds and swamps and through the mangrove trees. Just like I did, you will get sand in your eyes, mosquito bites, bitten by all types of centipedes and scorpions (both the insect type and human types). But you have to keep going.

Remember this: The Bible says that God dropped manna from Heaven and fed the Israelites in the desert. But in these modern days, God doesn't drop any manna from Heaven any more. I guess that there are too many people on Earth today to share in the few flakes of manna falling from Heaven. Everybody is economizing maybe even in Heaven. So, you've got to get out there and look for it yourself and help God to help you.

The Israelites were lucky. Today, some of us have to, in some way or the other, make luck come our way. At 97 years of age I am still trying to find that luck formula!

My father was a cook and pastry chef on many ships that sailed between the West Indies, South American countries, the United States and Canada. He was constantly travelling back and forth, so much so, that when I lived with my adopted mother, he would come home from one of his journeys and bring tons of stuff – food and clothes for me and everyone else.

When my brother Kenneth, was around 17 years of age, my father took him on several trips on the ships where he served as an assistant in the galley. Later on, my brother finally settled in Port of Spain, Trinidad and opened a tailor shop on Sackville Street.

My son, Marcus, recently found ships documents such as manifests and crew lists that document many of my father's trips as well as those of Kenneth. My father's and brother's actually wrote their names and family information on these manifests which show the names of both passengers and crew members. Marcus also found a picture on the internet of one of the ships my father worked on – The Canadian Otter!

My Childhood Days

Even though I grew up in the countryside, I treasure my childhood days. Why? They were far different from these days. Everyone looked out for each other. Everyone lived in unity. When children misbehaved, even the neighbors corrected them. And this was never a problem with their parents because they were doing the same thing with the neighbors' children.

In today's world, even in your own home, children cannot be corrected in the old ways... because it is against the law! And some parents don't focus on training children in their home – maybe because these parents don't have any home training themselves. If the parents don't have home training how can they correct children or raise them in the proper way?

However, my younger days were not all that easy particularly when I lived with my adopted mother. When your parents are not around – it can be a difficult thing for a child... even when other family members are around. I remember those days both with tears and smiles.

After my adopted mother's death, life turned out to be different. I was kind of on my own then. When I finished school, I worked as a school teacher – in the same school that I went to as a child. During this time, I also attended teacher training school and completed my first Teacher's Certificate and was working on my second when I emigrated.

Life is difficult when you are young, single and on your own. With literally only a few pence for a salary, I found myself fighting for survival. Plus, I wanted more out of life. My father was a travelling man who had seen the world. He had told me amazing stories of what life was like around the West Indies and the World.

So, like many other people in those days, I migrated to some of the other islands. For example, I had relatives in St. Vincent. My mother's uncle, Mr. Daisley was a School Master there. I stayed in St. Vincent with them for a while, but because I was not satisfied, I left and went to Grenada. Still not finding what I wanted, I went to Trinidad.

When I went to Trinidad, I met lots of cousins and other family members. A lot of my cousins were from my mother's side of the family, the Daisley's. My mother's uncle lived there and had 'tons' of children. Some of them were adopted by my aunt (my mother's sister) Daisy Daisley-Allumbey who had migrated to Tobago with her new husband.

In Trinidad, I stayed with one of my cousins, Daphne Mottley. I did not like Trinidad. Why? Back home in Barbados, I was a country girl. I went from school to home – to church – and back home. In Barbados, I had never ever entered a dance hall and was never allowed to go fetes and such things.

But in Trinidad, every night there were parties and dances – here, there and everywhere – all of which my cousins wanted to take me to. When I refused to go, I was told that no one came to Trinidad and 'play Christian.'

I was given a week to fall in line!

Well, I took off as fast as I could. No siree – that life was not for me. I left and went to St. Lucia where I had a few friends and family. By that time, my father had stopped sailing and had also moved to St. Lucia.

A Barbadian gentleman gave me a job in his drug store. But then the St. Lucian girls found out that I was not a creole girl and that I could not speak Patois, so that job was short lived. I guess they did not like me... I was too 'British' and 'proper' being from Barbados, which was also known as Little England.

Coming to Antigua

My father, being a travelling man, later decided to move to Antigua. He did not like to stay in one place too long. One of his favorite sayings was that a rolling stone gathers no moss! I guess I rolled right along with him because I have lived in Trinidad, St. Vincent, Grenada and St. Lucia.

He got a job in St. Johns working in a baker shop for a Barbadian man, down by where Mendes Store at the bottom of Redcliffe Street was (where Redcliffe Quay is now). He also used to cane the bottom of the chairs for Destin who had a joiner shop in Point.

So, I took the chance and migrated to Antigua. When I first came here I lived for a few months in the Point area. Then I moved to George Street, Greenbay. I lived at the corner close to where a man named Bungalow Brown (related to Studyation Brown) lived across the street from the Perry family (they owned the land at Perry's Bay). After that I rented a small house at Perry's Bay.

When my son was about three years of age and after my father died, I emigrated to St. Kitts and lived there for about six months. But life there was very difficult so I went back to Antigua and rented a small house on the road between Greenbay Moravian Church and Greenbay/Grays Farm cross roads. I next rented a house just off George Street in the area behind Clem's shop.

Well, folks say that life is how you make it. But I find that phrase a bit difficult to understand… especially for me… trying and trying and trying… and never made it to where I wanted it to be.

Manna was never dropped from Heaven for me. At least, I didn't find any.

But I think I realized why! I was in the right church but in the wrong pew. Most of the manna fell for those in the pews up front… White and light skinned people!

However, even though the scale refused to balance for me, it is good to be breathing the breath of life. Many millions of people have passed from time into eternity whether their scale was balanced or not! When I wake up to the sound of CNN or Aljazeera, I know that I am blessed.

Maybe that's how my scale was balanced… Long life and good health – not money! I'll take those rather than a short life – ill health and lots of money! Anyway – now I don't have a choice.

My health is my wealth! I am truly humbled and blessed! My blessings from Heaven came in the form of long life, good health, a great son, and a few good, supportive friends.

I have been here in Antigua making it my adopted home, the only island I seem to like! And having spent so much time here, and having raised a son here, it is fit to call it home. But interestingly enough, it amazes me, that even though I only spent my childhood and young adulthood in Barbados, I still feel strongly that that is my real home.

I am a Bajan through and through. Some people tell me that when I speak, they can still hear the Bajan twang in my voice! I guess what is in my heart sounds through my voice.

My Prayers

Why I Pray

Prayers are a fundamental part of my life. I don't think that I could have survived the last 75 years without prayers. I developed an early habit of praying based on what my father taught me.

My father travelled widely. But he also read widely. I guess when you are on one of those slow ships going from South America to North America… you have lots of time on your hands. My father used the time to read. And he read all kinds of books. But he was particularly interested in spiritual books.

My father was also deeply involved in both the Odd Fellows, the Masons and had an association with the Rosicrucians. So he had access to some deep information. He also had in his possessions some ancient books (Hebrew, Greek, Indian (Hindu and Sanskrit) that taught lessons about life and spirituality. He read them all and passed many of them down to me… So I read them all. And, of course, I made sure my son read them too and exposed him to the hidden knowledge of some of those secretive organizations.

So I learned a lot from and through my father. I learned the importance of spiritual discipline. And I learned the importance of prayer and its powerful benefits.

Through my early readings and teaching from my father, I developed both knowledge and skills that allowed me to help and give guidance to a lot of people throughout my years.

If anything, prayer is the one thread that has kept my life on an even keel. When things did not go well… my answer was prayer. When I did not know where my next meal was coming from… prayer showed me the way. When I did not know where I would get my next dollar from I got my inspiration from prayer. When people stood against me and blocked my path, prayer opened the way. When hurricanes and floods brought destruction to my little hut – prayer helped me to rebuild a little bigger and a lot better. When debt threatened and when I needed cash suddenly… through prayer I received more than the needed blessings.

From nothing – prayer brought me plenty. Like the Good Book says… the birds don't worry about food for the next day… neither do the ants or bees… they take care of today. Tomorrow will take care of itself. Prayer has given me that mindset. It is cemented in my being.

And it is not only prayer. It is belief in the prayer. It is the constant praying. It is the knowledge that prayer works. It is the confidence that prayer works. It is confidence that comes from experience of success.

How prayer works is a mystery.

But the fact that it works is no mystery. How to pray is also no mystery. What to say when I pray is no mystery. How to say it when I pray is no mystery.

Let me emphasize: The fact that prayer works is no mystery!

Just pray!

Pray with strong feeling. Pray with energy. Pray with strong belief. Pray with intensity.

Pray with belief… belief that that which you ask for is done. It is fulfilled. See it happening. Feel it happening. Taste it happening. Smell the sweet smell of success. Rejoice that it has happened. Be Strong. Be Powerful. Be Intense.

Pray as if nothing else mattered.

Other Selected Thoughts on Prayer

- When I pray, I pray as if my prayers are already answered. I act as if my prayers are already answered. I talk as if my prayers are already answered. However, this is easy to say but harder to do… very, very hard to do.

- We must see our prayers come true and come through. And we must feel them as if they had already come through.

- Again, as I have always said I believe in prayer… and I have seen it work in wondrous ways. For example, the police was looking for a man in St. Vincent. The man came to my father for a prayer of protection. My father gave him an interesting prayer involving three special words of power.

  When the police came to the home… the man was sitting on a stone in the family's yard. I was there that day and saw it happen. The man started to silently repeat the prayer. The police passed right by him… asking everyone for his whereabouts.

Now these were policemen who were from the same village and knew the man by sight. But on that day their eyes were blinded by his belief in his prayer... and by the power of that three word prayer. Son, keep those three words in your mental vault. And pass them on to your sons when they are ready...

- When we pray we must not be too impatient in looking for results. And we must not mistake the signs of incoming answers or events for the real thing. When you put milk to boil... how long it takes will depend on the strength of the fire and the amount of milk in the pot. With prayer, you should have strong internal fire and passion, mixed with unyielding faith and confidence. The more you want... the stronger and more intense the mix needs to be.

Let me repeat: When you pray... how long the results take to come into being will depend on the strength of your belief and faith and the size of your desire. If you look at the pot of milk as you wait for it to boil... it seems as if it takes a long time. Then you begin to notice some movement on the surface. This movement is not the milk boiling... it is the sign that the milk is about to boil. So... you don't remove it from the fire at that point.

When you pray, you may often get some signs that the prayer is being answered. For example... you may pray for a blessing of a $1000. And when you get $50 in the mail you become very disappointed. Well... the $50 is the first sign of movement toward your $1000.... If you doubt the efficacy of prayer, lose confidence in your ability to pray, or give up now (like taking the pot off the fire) you will never get your ultimate desire ($1000)! Stay with it... keep praying! Accept the appetizers... ($50)... and keep praying... your main meal may go way beyond what you ordered from the Ultimate Chef.

- We have to be fear-less rather than fear-ful! Throughout my life... as I look back, many of the things that I have done were not done out of fear but out of positive and intense desire. All of my actions showed this... I awoke every morning with powerful prayers... "I shall not be afraid of the terror by night... nor of the bullet that flies by day... nor of the pestilence that walks in the darkness... nor of the destruction that lays waste at noon day."

(From Psalm 91). We must walk in this world with courage showing in every step… We must prepare for and face both the seen and unseen dangers that are about us. We must look the 'thief' in the eye… and dare him and then scare him! We must not step back or step around… but we must step through and step on! We must face not with fear but with inner faith and inner force! "The young lion and the serpent shall I trample."

- This inner faith and force is an attitude that stems from a firm determination to be the master and mistress of my world! I will not back down from anything that this world throws at me! I <u>will</u> the world to my way… to do my bidding! That has been my attitude. That is my attitude. And that will be my attitude… wherever I next go to!

- I used prayer as food. I prayed when I awoke. I prayed for breakfast. I prayed for lunch. I prayed for dinner. I prayed for supper. And prayer was my snack before I went to sleep. I still pray. But not like those days. In those days… when I didn't have much food… I filled myself up with prayer. And was satisfied at the meal.

- Don't watch and pray as the Bible says. Instead, you should WALK and pray. 'Manna' doesn't drop in your lap from Heaven these days… you have to walk and find it… and sometimes you have to walk for a long time. And even when you find it… you still have to work long hours to get it. While you are doing all of that… you should keep praying. And if you don't find any manna… then make some!

- Pray and believe. The doubter obtains nothing.

- Praying is not begging God! I don't beg. I pray. I ask! I request. I may even demand! But… people must understand that praying is not begging.

- When I pray… I have faith that my prayers will be answered. But we must accompany faith with works… and so before, during and after I pray… I work hard to help my prayers to come through.

- Don't ask for a miracle and prepare for trouble, disaster or disease! A part of your prayer for success is the act of preparing for the success that you want… and when it comes don't act surprised.

- Faith and belief is the issue here… and it has to be demonstrated. You must act 'as if' what you have asked for has already come true and come through.

According to the Good Book, Faith is the assurance of things hoped for and the conviction of things not seen. It also says to call those things that be not… as if they be!

I have chosen a few prayers out of my long list of special prayers and have listed them below.

My Personal Prayer of Protection

The blessing that came from Heaven, from God the Father, when the true living Son was born, be with me Hyacinth Mottley.

The blessing that God spoke over the whole human race be with me Hyacinth Mottley always.

The Holy Cross of God, as long and as broad as the one on which God suffered his bitter torture, bless me Hyacinth Mottley today and for ever more.

The bitter crown of thorns which was forced upon the holy head of Jesus Christ, bless me today and forever.

The three holy nails which were driven through the Holy hands and feet of Jesus Christ, bless me Hyacinth Mottley today and forever.

The spear by which the Holy side of Jesus was opened, bless me today and forever.

The rosy blood protect me from ally my enemies and from everything that might be injurious to my body or soul, or my worldly goods.

Bless me, oh ye five holy wounds, in order that all my enemies may be driven away and bound.

As well as the cup and wine that Jesus gave unto his disciples on noon day Thursday.

All those who hate me Hyacinth Mottley must be silent before me. Their hearts are dead in regards to me and their tongues are mute so that they cannot inflict the least injury upon me or my house or my premises. Likewise all those who attempt attacking me, with their arms or weapons, shall be made weak and defenseless and conquered before me Hyacinth Mottley.

In the name of God the Father, God the Son, and God the Holy Spirit, Amen.

A Prayer of Reverence

The Cross of Christ be with me Hyacinth Mottley.
The Cross of Christ overcome all water and every fire.
The Cross of Christ overcome all weapons.
The Cross of Christ is a perfect sign and blessing to my soul.

Now I pray, I Hyacinth Mottley pray that God the Father, for the Soul's sake, and I pray God the Son for the Father's sake, and I pray God the Holy Ghost for the Father and the Son's sake, that the Holy Corpse of God, may bless me against all evil things, words and works.

The Cross of Christ opens unto me future blessings.

The Cross of Christ be with me, above me, beneath me, aside of me, before all my enemies – visible and invisible, and everywhere.

They all flee as soon as they hear Enoch and Elias, these two prophets were never imprisoned beaten or bound. Thus none of mine enemies may be able to injure of attack me in my life or my body.

In the name of God the Father, God the Son and God the Holy Spirit. Amen.

Prayer for Success

I affirm that I am now in the orbit of success. I am surrounded by a magnetic field of positive life force.

My mind is now programmed with success. I must overcome all my difficulties.

I am in the magic circle of God's divine love. Thus, no man's hands can stop me from being successful in my undertakings, that I may be well blessed and that no unjust verdict may ever be rendered against me Hyacinth Mottley.

In the name of God the Father, God the Son and God the Holy Spirit.

Amen.

Prayer for Formidable Assistance

In the name of God I do begin.

Lame your hands and feet because you sin.

God grant that I may come out best or never I will find peace or rest.

In the name of God the Father, God the Son, and God the Holy Spirit.

Amen.

More About Praying

It doesn't make any sense that you are going to pray for something if you are not going to believe. If you don't believe and if you don't believe strongly – then you might as well not bother praying.

Prayer works. I know that because I have experienced it all the time... all the days of my life with success. I pray fervently for something and it shows up. After I was thrown on my own as a young girl, I never had anyone to give me anything – so I relied solely and only on prayer.

Here in Antigua, I know people who wanted a job and couldn't get any. I used prayer to get what I wanted including work. If you want a job pick up one... just like that... through prayer! Prayer with powerful belief works... all the time.

When to pray? I pray morning, noon and night... there is no special time to pray. Sometimes, of course, you need to say a special prayer for a special desire. But most importantly, you should be praying all the time for general blessings... for health, wealth and to stave off bad influences. Always pray for protection as a prevention to stop bad things from happening before they start and before they get a foothold in your life. When everybody else suffering – you just keep going… and as you go… you pray. On the other hand, pray as you go – in order to keep going!

These are not the days when you can kneel and pray… These are the days when you have to ask as you pray, seek as you pray… and knock and keep busy as you pray. I am not waiting for anything to drop in my lap… I go after it with plenty prayer as fuel. God helps those who help themselves!

Prayer is the engine, the fuel, the wheels and the vehicle that I drive… and that drives me.

Seeking after what you want is the most important thing. You can ask God for anything and sit down and wait for it to come. But… you might be sitting and waiting for a long time.

If you are a farmer, you have to plow the ground, plant your seeds and begin to carry water to the ground – while you pray for rain to help lighten your load. If you are a fisherman and you throw out your line and the fish are not biting… throw down a net and catch them… and if that doesn't work... get some dynamite like they used to do in the old days!

Pray With Your Legs

I read somewhere that a former slave (Frederick Douglass) said the following: "I prayed for twenty years (as a slave) but received no answer until I prayed with my legs."

When I was a child the adults and the preachers used to tell us to watch and pray. But I can tell you that I don't watch and pray... I walk and pray! And even now that I am not walking like I used to... I pray as I go... I pray as I sit... I pray as I lie in bed... I pray all the time – morning, noon and night.

And, that is how you should pray.

I read somewhere else that "Practical prayer is harder on the soles of your feet than on the knees." I guess that is for those who walk as they pray... rather than those who kneel as they pray.

Sometimes you are walking and you are praying... and you don't exactly know where you are going... and all of a sudden somebody says, "Hey, me just hear that so and so want a maid!" All of a sudden the job that you were walking and praying for shows up – just like that. Just like that slave: Frederick Douglass.

I remember when I got my first job in Antigua, as I was walking and asking people if they knew if anybody had a job for a maid, somebody told me that a woman in Ovals needed a maid. As I was headed over there, I met a good friend of mine… Gus Alloway… who told me: "No go over dey… that a go be a difficult woman foo work for." Instead she told me about another job with a family in the same Ovals area close to East Street below Michael's Mount. I got that job and worked with that family for a good while doing mostly cooking.

My Life in Antigua

Working in Antigua

Things were rough back in those days. I worked for $3 per week in my first job with the family over on East Street below Michael's Mount… just $3. But it was enough to keep me and my son alive.

I think that the members of this family were descendants from the British and their father was in charge of an Estate. One of their older sons got a job in a bank and the family added another dollar to my pay to $4 per week. That was a big raise!

I left that job not knowing where I would get another one. But I walked away. However, when I walked away… I was walking and I praying all the time. And someone whispered to me about another job with a family with a Portuguese name who lived on High Street. But I didn't stay there long because they wanted slaves not servants. I was a paid staff not a paid slave.

What's the difference: I am in control of whether I stay or go! There are things that as a paid staff I won't do. There are ways you can talk to slaves – that I won't accept as a paid staff. I am equal to anyone and must be treated as an equal. That is my thinking now and it was my thinking back in those days.

People must understand that I was ashamed of having to work in somebody's house in order to make a living. I was afraid that someday someone from Barbados would get to know that a "Mottley" was working as a servant in Antigua.

Only one person in Antigua knew of my family back in Barbados. That person was Ethlyn Drayton (now deceased). She was not only Barbadian, but she was a distant cousin. She was the only person from Barbados who knew my status here.

I believe that I was a little different from some of the other women who used to do the same kinds of work.

I am an independent spirit. I was raised to be independent. I don't depend on people. I am my own mistress and master. I never liked the word 'servant' – not because of the work – but because of what the people who you worked for thought it meant. They acted as if it meant paid 'slave'.

Well – all it meant for me – was that I worked and they paid me. That's it… nothing more… nothing less. I was equal to them in every way. And to tell you the truth, some of the people I worked with had just a little more money than I did… but they acted as if they were lords and ladies. As I worked with these families, I got to know how they lived, how they thought, how they made money, and all kinds of things I would rather leave alone.

So I lived my life independently… if I didn't like how the so called 'master' or 'mistress' talked to me… or if I didn't like what they wanted me to do… I walked away and found another job. I had the firm belief that I could get work anytime I wanted to. Why? Because I had prayer on my lips and God in my heart… all the time.

I was poor… but I was high minded. Yes… my status in Antigua was not high… I didn't have money… Sometimes, I had to scrounge to make ends meet… but I was high minded. As I said before I didn't want anyone from my home in Barbados to know that I was doing servant work in Antigua… and I was determined that I would make it on my own… and make a living independently. And I carried my 'high mindedness' everywhere… no matter where I worked or for whom I worked.

I even worked for several months as a servant in V.C. Bird's house when they lived in the area they now call Radio Range where the old ABS Radio Station was located. That was an experience working for that family!

It was an experience working for all of those families… particularly as you look at them now and listen to the children some of whom are now 'big shots' in Antigua. I know a lot about many of those families from the inside – how they grew up – what the day to day struggles and drama were – their values and morals and what really went on. I know these things for myself… and from other maids who worked with these and other families.

But that is life… and all those things are private and confidential… no one can pluck that information from me… My son knows all those stories… but he too will keep those things to himself. These are life's lessons… and every family has its history – some good… some not so good… and it is really nobody's business.

But it is interesting to reflect on where people were, what they were doing… and how some of them have made it through struggles that were similar to mine. The difference is some of them made it big… but it wasn't beautiful. It was hard – even for them – the so-called 'big shots'.

1950 Hurricane

That 1950 hurricane was terrible. I think it was the second hurricane within a couple weeks of each other. My son was just two weeks old and my father was sick in bed. He had had a stroke and was not in good shape.

We lived at Perry's Bay – right by the beach. During the hurricane water came from Ovals, Ottos, and Grays Hill right down to the beach at Perry's Bay. Water came into the house and rose up to the windows. I prayed and I prayed and I prayed. Suddenly somebody knocked on one of the windows.

When I opened it water rushed in! Outside was a neighbor – Cyril King and his son – Ivan. They saved us that day. To this day I don't know why they even thought of us. But they did. I believe that, once again, my prayers worked as I believed they would. But… with that water rising in the house so quickly… it was close!

Starting My Own Business

I wanted to get away from being a 'servant' in other people's houses. So, after my father died (as a result of a stroke), I put my little pennies together and bought soaps and combs and other trinkets. My idea was to sell around the area. But one of my friends introduced me to a man named Mr. Hector in Liberta. He suggested that I come to Liberta on Sundays and sell my things to people.

So every Sunday, I packed a little suitcase and took the bus to Liberta. Mr. Hector introduced me to his neighbors and they began to purchase some of my items. I walked all over that village and then walked out to New Village also. I developed a lot of customers.

Although the money I made from this was 'small change', it was still a lot better than $3 or $4 a week. Much better. And, I was independent and in business for myself. That was important to me.

One day, a customer told me that she didn't have all the money to buy what she wanted, and she asked me if I would credit her until when I came again. I told her yes… and after that, when people found out that I gave credit, my business expanded quickly. Now all kinds of people wanted to buy my things. Some people even ordered items from me. I guess it was easier for me to bring them stuff than if they had to get on the bus and go to town to buy it for themselves! I didn't mind crediting it to them!

Then I got the idea to go 'Round South' to those villages – Crabbs Hill, Johnson's Point, Urlings and sometimes… Old Road. One Sunday I would go to Liberta, Falmouth and English Harbor… and the other Sunday I would go 'Round South'.

Business was good but it was hard going. And everywhere I went I took my son with me. At that time he was probably between five and seven. I was not going to leave him to get knocked about by other people. Even up to as recently as five years ago, I met an old woman from Urlings who remembered me and asked me – "Whey dee little boy?" That little boy is now 61 years old!

My Specialty

A special request by one of my customers put me on a lifelong path in another business area.

One of my regular customers told me that she didn't have any money on that day, but that she badly wanted a comb and if I could credit it to her. So I did. She showed it to one of her friends who promptly advised her to return it to me quickly "Because that Bajan woman no mek no joke… If you owe she and no pay she – 'she go do for you'!"

Another woman asked me if I had any remedy for a particular problem she was having. I told her that I could get it for her. The next Sunday I gave it to her and apparently it worked well.

The word spread quickly that I 'could do things' and that I 'could help people'. I don't exactly know how or from whom, but people got the idea that I knew a little 'mysticism'. I began to get requests for all types of assistance from people all over Antigua. I realized then, that my father had trained me well all those years ago.

My father was what you could call a 'faith healer'. As a man who travelled around the world on ships, he had learned a lot of things about prayer, faith and healing. He had seen how people from far off places used their beliefs to heal people of really terrible diseases, disorders and all sorts of types of strange afflictions.

Over the years, as I travelled with him around the Caribbean, he had taught me things that he had learned and told me stories about healing prayers and about herbs and other substances that native and local people used to great benefit to help themselves. These things are too much to put in this book.

I hope that God spare me the time so that I can share them in another book with the general public. If I do not, I hope my son will. I have taught him all that I know… he doesn't use much of that information… but he can help me to share it with you the reader.

So, now, here I was in Antigua, trying to make a living by selling little of this and a little of that, and people have started to ask me to help them with their troubling problems.

Once the word got around, people started to come to my home requesting my services. Eventually, I gave up the travelling and selling to concentrate on helping people.

Now, I have to tell you that it wasn't easy because I had to tell some people "No" and turn them away. Why? Because some people had all kinds of evil requests to do harm to other people. For many of them, I had to be clear… "I help people – I don't hurt people. Don't come to me asking me to do anything evil or negative."

I wasn't not going to put my spirit and soul in jeopardy with God by trying to help them in their evil and negative desires.

Just like I am doing here in this book, I taught people about the power of prayer. I taught them which prayers were good for which issues. I helped them with herbal healings. I helped them with spiritual blessings based on Christian teachings and principles. I counseled them with regards to their work, their relationships, their family, their finances and their friends. I gave them counseling about life.

It was a joy to do this work. I knew I was helping people to be the best they could be and to get the most out of life that was possible for them. I felt blessed when someone came by with tears of joy testifying about how helpful my intervention or assistance was.

I also felt honored when people shared their most intimate secrets, their most difficult struggles, their deepest fears and their most troubling worries.

In doing this work, I have been honored to try my hand at helping rich and poor, powerful and downtrodden, politician and preacher, doctor and nurse, teacher and student, mother and father, children and grandchildren, Antiguan and foreigner.

In all of this, I still considered myself as a staff... but now the only masters I served were God and people. I was now totally independent. Working for myself – being my own boss was exciting and freeing. My work often took me overseas particularly to the Virgin Islands where I had quite a few clients!

Words & Thoughts To My Son

Words & Thoughts To My Son

- One of your letters said that it will be easy to get a degree – providing you stay with it for the whole time. What do you mean? I thought you intended to stay until you are through. I thought it was a degree or degrees that you are fighting for. You don't lose your mind and blow the scene, O.K.? However, you know your business best. I want for you a B.A., M.A., Ph.D., Dr… in whatever field. Strive for it… however, and wherever it goes. September 6th, 1984.

- Marcus… when I came across all those university catalogs, I realized how many universities you had written to over so many years starting way back when you worked for LIAT (early 1970's) and when you were teaching (late 1970s). University in Oregon, University in California, University in Georgia, University in Canada, Howard University in Washington, D.C., University in New York, University in Texas… Universities all over – even Birmingham and London. Now you are in Washington, D.C. at Howard University. God really worked a miracle of you… trust in him. March 4, 1985.

- When you pray be careful of how you respond to what you get. I read somewhere that if you pray for rain… don't complain about the mud!

- Ask for Divine guidance, then, make the best choice of those colleges. Now that you are there, visit them if you can… and for those that are far away, call them on the telephone. Make the best choice and then go for it with all that you have. Once you get there – work as hard as you can… and then work even harder. April 1986.

- You have spent all of your time and your youth here (in Antigua). And, now that you are there in the U.S. make up for what you have been missing. Despite the fact that you are all I have… don't make me hinder you. It is imperative that you make a place for yourself. Get all the education, knowledge and experience that you want. Read all the books that you can. Just as Solomon asked God for knowledge, understanding and wisdom, so you must go out there and get all that you can.   May 23rd, 1985.

- Keep a cool head and handle yourself wisely. June 4th, 1985.

- Whatever you have to do… practice doing it right away. "Don't put off until tomorrow what you can do today." And, don't waste time. Don't 'lime'. I once read that "Killing time is not murder. It is suicide." Time is the only thing that you have to get what you want and to build and create your dream. Waste time and you waste your life. November 11th, 1985.

- I cannot wait to hear your logic on mysticism, astral travelling, clairvoyance and so on. As old as I am, I am here to learn and to add to my know-how. Yes, I meditate, but these days I can't seem to get that powerful inner feeling of tranquility that I had experienced in the past. I know you are secretly becoming an expert at these things. Keep them to yourself… no one must know of your inner skill… inner calm and inner power. Practice secretly. No one. No one must know. Jan 17, 1986.

UFOs: Today (September 3rd, 1987), the radio said that last night Unidentified Flying Objects were seen the southern part of the island. A police man in his police car on the Valley Church Road saw this big ball of illuminating light as big as the moon flying over head with a long tail. The lights were yellow and green and the lights were such as he never saw before. He said it was if it was trailing his car. Then suddenly, it stopped moving – just staying there. It then took off towards Darkwood, as if it wanted to land, but it did not. Instead it went to the Five Island area, then in the direction of Coolidge and then it disappeared. That was in the local news.

Then the regional news came on saying that people in Barbados saw a UFO flying over there. A restaurant owner saw it and called out the people inside (the restaurant) to see. There were eleven people in all who saw it. They described it as a big ball of illuminating light with a long tail cruising around. Then it divided itself and added four parts. So instead of seeing one big ball you saw five lights sparkling with long tails.

Then the news said that people in St. Lucia saw the same thing flying over their island. But the news did not describe it.

Apparently we are having visitors. This is very amusing to me. I have always been interested in UFO's. There are a lot of things in this world that we can't explain.

- In your life be careful with insurance companies. They are supposed to be paying me some money… but it has been months now and I haven't received anything. They hassle you for money… to pay them. But when it's your time to collect… they avoid you like the plague. When I get my money, they won't catch me again! February 16th, 1988.

- When you start something… don't stop. Don't stop unless you outgrow it. Don't stop until you succeed! And don't go after it with a little… go after it with a lot… with all of you! And, when you get tired keep going… uphill, downhill… or even if have to swim. June 21st, 1988.

- I didn't get any mansions in Antigua. But from where I started… even a one room house is like a palace. As difficult as it was, did I imagine that I could make it through to the little bit that I have now? Yes… I imagined it… and I believed it… and I worked hard to move to it. No one else had to believe… and there was no one else to believe in me… except you… and I know that you did. My belief in myself and knowing that my life was in my own hands… and your life was in my hands… kept me going through thick and thin… through all the difficult times. My imagination of what I could do and how I could do it kept me alive and moving forward every day. August 15th, 1988.

- Keep learning. It is important to gather knowledge. Then get understanding. Then apply your understanding and your knowledge. Do that often enough and you will get wisdom. The main portion is in doing what you have to do. Don't just focus on knowledge… focus your time on doing something with your knowledge. November 23rd, 1988.

- 'Count your blessings, name them one by one! Count your blessings, see what God has done…' in your life! It is important to remember the powerful and good things in your life particularly when times are dark.

Health

Health

If we don't take care of ourselves no one else will. I will not wait on God or man to take care of me. God will help me if I help myself. So I am a great believer in vitamins, I eat lots of ground provision (potatoes, yams, eddoes (taro)), bread fruit, spinach, okro, peas and beans (all kinds), and eddoe tops (taro leaves). I don't particularly love chicken or red meat... I love fish. Pepperpot is one of my favorites. I don't like too much sugar, salt, butter or sweet oil (cooking oil). I also love my herb tea!

(The following are excerpted from letters to my son.)

- I take my tablets and vitamins and I try to relax every day. August 29th, 1984.

- I am none of the best... and none of the worst. I take my medication every day. I meditate, do the breathing exercise and do some exercises that I see on TV. January 29th, 1985.

- I go to the doctor every month so that I can check my pressure and examine everything. Sometimes the nurse from the Grays Farm clinic comes to my home and checks my pressure. This is a health habit (checking your pressure and your sugar) that you must develop and carry into your old age. I don't like these drug medications... but if they keep me alive... then I will live long. So... I take them.

- I believe strongly in self healing. I have seen it when I was a little girl and my father told me many stories about people who healed themselves.

Physic Nut

A married woman brought her sister who is single to see me. The unmarried sister hates men because she says she is not lucky with them. The married sister's husband is in New York and he filed for her to become a US citizen. She says that she got through and would be going up soon.

However, she complained about him saying that he was too possessive, he was too mean, and that he noticed everything. When she said that to her sister (the one that's single), she encouraged her to leave him and if she couldn't leave him that she advised that she should poison him. And the sister told her how to do it. She advised her to get some physic nut, and to give him a little at a time. She said that would make him vomit, and vomit and no doctor would be able to find out what was wrong with him. What terrible people… they don't understand that what you do to others you are really doing to yourself. It will boomerang back to them – or their children – for generations to come!

I know physic nut from Barbados as a child. It is a tree that bears a fruit that the old people used to tell us that the Bible calls the forbidden fruit.

Now, I am just trying to make a point. When I hear things, I don't pass them by. You shouldn't either. Listen carefully to what people say… especially when they are talking about other people. Remember that they won't tell you how they really feel about you. But you can understand them by what they say about others.

I am 75 years old. I know that plant, and I have known it since I was a child. But, it is the first that I am hearing that people use it to damage other people.

My mind goes back to Mrs. _____ (an old friend). I believe that is her problem… she vomits and vomits and vomits… and the doctors don't know and can't find out what's wrong. Somebody did that to her!

Son, my point is that when you come back to Antigua be careful even of those who you think are your best friends. Don't eat or drink too freely.

Every shadow is a gun. We have a saying that "to live is to learn". But I am telling you that you must "Learn to live!"

I may sound boring, but everything is knowledge. This little piece of information about the physic nut is not politics. It is not what's taking place in the private sector.

But, it is what can hurry house one to their long home.

So… memorize that piece of information about the physic nut. (June 11, 1989)

Turkey Berry Tree

My father once told me that he had a friend who was healed and cured from 'stoppage of water' by using the leaves and the berry of the 'Clamman Cherry Tree.' We have all kinds of helpful things around us (plants) that we really don't know how to use until some 'white man' put it in a tablet, charge us 'an arm and leg' and tell us that "it's good for everything!"

Social Life & Politics

Relationships: *Respect Yourself*

I think that being my own boss added years to my life. It kept me refreshed and rejuvenated. I avoided the mistakes that I saw some of my clients and neighbors making.

One of the things that I avoided was having stupid relationships with men. My son's father was a no-good man. When I became pregnant he disappeared until long after my son was born. So when he wanted to come around again – I drove him off. And, except for one, I drove off the rest of them that tried to come around.

So many of the women that I knew (both Antiguan and foreign) had 'ninety-eleven' 'picanie': some for this man, some for that man… and some for Tom, Dick and Harry. Instead of going and looking for work to do… to make their own money and control their own lives… they ended up depending on one no-good man after another… and being disappointed every time.

Not me… no way… That was not going to happen to me more than once. I had one child and his father ran away from his responsibility. I met him on the street, holding his child and did not even look at him. I was not going to let that happen to me again. So I had only one child. I was OK with that! Rather than depend on men like this, I chose to go into people's houses and wash their pot and cook their food – working in this way for a living!

I was proud. I was independent. I was high minded. And my upbringing taught me good values. No man was going to use me as their 'play-ting'.

People all over, including those in Perry's Bay, call me Ms. Mottley. They always called me Ms. Mottley. That was because no one had anything negative to say about me. I didn't have any man running in and out of my house. My name was not on the women's tongues. Instead everybody respected me. They didn't have anything bad to whisper or say out loud… so they stuck to treating me respectfully.

I respected myself first… and they followed my lead. That's how people should manage their lives. Respect yourself before you expect others to respect you.

Friendships

I had one good friend in Antigua – Gus Alloway. People used to say all kinds of bad things about her. I disagree with them. While she wasn't a saint, she also wasn't a prostitute or anything close to that. What I can say is that she was quick to speak her mind… and would do so anywhere… in the shop… in the street… or even in church. But she was a good person – at least to me. She was the only person I could talk to and get solid advice from. She knew everybody in Antigua and because of that she could give me good counsel on who to avoid and how to approach people.

She died a long time ago… and over the years, I have not really had any other friend who I could talk with like we did.

It is not easy to come to a new island and develop friends that one can trust. You really don't know who is who. So, except for her, I avoided making close friends with people.

A person has to be special for you to share your real feelings and thoughts with. They have to have shown you all sides of them for you to make a decision if to trust them and bring them closer or if to keep them at a distance.

As I have counseled people here in Antigua and elsewhere, I find that too many people are not discerning when they develop friendships. They tell their business to anyone and everyone. And of course, they always live to regret doing so. I always tell my son, "Don't make your left hand know what your right hand is doing." You can't get any closer than your left hand and right hand… That means that telling another person your real story, your real feelings, your real thoughts – must be a very rare occasion and then only to a very special, proven person. As they say… "Keep your own counsel." That is why people pay lawyers and psychologists… because they are duty bound to keep secrets!

Poverty

I think that poverty is a disease. According to the Bible the only type of poverty that is sanctioned by God is to be poor in spirit. Drought is not a natural state of things in nature – except maybe in the desert. Similarly, poverty is not a natural state for humans either. Or... it shouldn't be.

Back in the days when I came to Antigua everybody was poor. But you could stretch the little money that we got... even if it was only $3 per week. I was poor... dirt poor. But I wasn't poor in spirit! In that I was very rich. I was very hopeful. I was very determined. And I was very focused on the fact that I would do whatever I could to make ends meet and beyond.

I knew it would be an uphill task. But I also knew that I had God on my side and that prayer was my connection to everything that I wanted. But it must be understood that my focus on God and my focus on prayer was not all. I was determined that I would do the hard work that I needed to do to make ends meet, take care of my son, keep food on the table, and keep a roof over our heads.

While my neighbors were busy quarreling with each other and minding each other's business, I was busy – quietly minding my own business. No one knew what I was doing or what I was thinking. When things were rough – only God and I knew it. When things got better... only God and I knew it. I kept people out of my business.

However, when I built a little house people's tongues started wagging. And, then when I expanded that house a little bigger their tongues literally caught on fire. When I my son started going to St. Joseph's Academy – their tongues took off. "Whey she get money for send he to tha school dey?" "A wha she a do dong dey?" "She a work 'obeah'! A 'obeah' woman she be." But when they met me at the stand pipe or in the coals market... they called me Ms. Mottley!

They should have asked me. Prayer was 'my refuge and my fortress'. My daily prayer no matter what it was – was really about one foremost thing: "Give me this day my daily bread." And after that I prayed for my son to be blessed.

I also prayed that we be showered with safety and security. But I locked my door at night and kept a dog in the yard.

Thoughts on Money

My father taught me many things as I was growing up and even when I was a young adult. I learned about the places that he had travelled to, the customs of the people whom he had met and many of the wonderful things that he had seen and learned.

He taught me about the power of prayer and encouraged me to read the many strange and powerful spiritual books that he had collected in his travels. He introduced me to techniques and practices that I, in turn, have used to help thousands of people.

But there is one lesson that I learned from him that has stayed with me beyond many of the others. "Save your pennies when you are young because you are going to need them in your old age." Now he didn't teach me that by what he said. He taught me that by the way he lived his life and by what he didn't have in his old age.

My father lived his life traveling on ships and going from here to there and everywhere else. He also lived loose and free with his money.

I can say that as a child, I had a lot of clothes and shoes because each time he came back home, he brought lots of clothing and other things for us. In that way, and in his way, he tried to take care of me and my brother.

But he was loose with his money and spent it on women and friends. As a matter of fact somewhere along the line, he had married another woman. She was a Royer, a Dominican who lived in Trinidad. I guess that marriage did not last long because he certainly did not have that part of his life in control or in good shape or perspective.

The bottom line is that he lived his life the way he wanted. But in doing so, he failed to plan for his old age. By the time he was old and sick, he did not have a penny in his name. So I had the responsibility for my young son and for him. It was a real struggle… but he was my father… he was my obligation.

One definition of happiness that I have is that happiness is often the lack of worry… particularly money worry. I have learned that to avoid money worry one has to be frugal. There is an old saying: "Waste not want not." People seem to have forgotten this.

Just about every day, I get both headache and heartache when I see the kinds of things that end up in the garbage, the amount of food being wasted, the coins that lie around, (some end up in the garbage too), and the way money is spent on the things that we can easily do without.

Some people might ask why they should do without some of these luxuries. But that is the wrong idea because it is not so much that they should do without luxuries. No it is not about luxuries, it is about preparing for a 'rainy day.' It is about being safe and secure. It is about having something put aside for the difficult times. And, you can call these days… right now… January 2012 – difficult times! People are losing their jobs. Many governments around the world – including Antigua – can't pay their workers. Even the banks who are supposed to be keeping your money don't have any. I can't even begin to imagine that. These days it might make more sense to keep your money in your mattress like we used to do in the old days!

Debt

I know that the world today seems to run on debt. Everybody has a debt problem including the so-called richest countries. This is a terrible situation where everyone is encouraged to borrow and borrow and borrow without any attention to how and when they are going to pay back the money they owe.

If people would be satisfied with what they have, and stop coveting other people's riches and running after a bigger house and a better car... they would be happier and live longer. I am not saying that people shouldn't try to grow in wealth... but most people over do it. All the focus is on getting richer and quicker. That's also why there are so many corrupt politicians and Antigua and elsewhere. Too much borrowing... and when they can't borrow anymore or at the level they want... they still have to get... so they end up stealing us blind. When the politicians steal... everybody else follow them.

So regarding the debt situation, I don't like to lend and I don't like to borrow.

When you lend people things – they turn around and make you enemy when you ask that your things be returned or for pay back. And some people keep borrowing and borrowing but they never have anything to share. These people are takers. And they will borrow you blind (or 'thief you blind') without any 'conscience'.

My attitude about not lending has caused me a few enemies in Antigua. Antiguans are a 'beggie beggie people'… even the government. They go and borrow from here and borrow from there. And now… they can't pay back. It's a good thing Stanford is in jail because he would own all of Antigua by now. Even the politicians beg you for your vote and when it's time for them to payback or give you a return on your vote… they are nowhere to be seen – until the next election.

If I won't lend… then I won't borrow. I don't want anyone washing their mouth over me because they had to lend me something.

We have a saying that "A fool and his money are soon parted." It applies particularly to poor people who are not accustomed to having money so when they get it…

particularly when they get a large sum… they spend and spend and spend until it's all gone.

I also learned that there is wisdom in "saving for a rainy day." I have had many dark, difficult and rainy days in my life. But the pennies that I had saved… turned around and saved me!

Tithing

There is one thing that I have used throughout my life as a guide: the principle and practice of tithing. The only difference between your understanding of tithing and mine is that I keep what I am tithing to God in my own bank account!

For every dollar that I earn, my practice was to tithe (save) at least 30 cents. That means that I do this even if I have to sacrifice something important. Why? Because I saw saving money as the most important financial activity. I worked – not to spend – but to save! No I never made any large amounts of money… so what I saved was small. But my little savings made me feel comfortable and I slept well at night.

Now imagine if Antigua and Barbuda had tithed to itself all those years…

Family

Family is very important. One of my regrets is that, because of my traveling to and fro, island hopping, I did not stay connected with my family roots. I have tons of family in Barbados, St. Vincent and Trinidad. I probably also have lots of family in New York and other parts of the US and England where many of the Mottley's, Daisley's and the Rouse's emigrated to in the early 1900's.

I had many cousins (Mottley's) who migrated to Trinidad. And my brother, Kenneth Mottley also migrated there and started a family. I also have a cousin (on my mother's side) – Daisy Daisly-Allumbey who migrated to Tobago!

All those other Mottley's in Barbados (including the lawyers and politicians) – as far as I understand, are also related.

I encourage everyone to pay attention to family connections. Although a lot of difficulties can come because of things some members of your family do, the benefits often outweigh the troubles. I know that some people have had some terrible experiences, but 'when push comes to shove' – sometimes the only people you have left to lean on are the members of your family.

For most of my life, I did not have a family umbrella here in Antigua since it was just me and my son. However, at my age now, I have family around me who care and who have shown me their love. I also have many friends who have shown and continue to show how much they care for me.

Some wise person said that "it is not flesh and blood alone that makes family… it is the heart." So, the lesson in this is that if you don't have family around you, you need to adopt one! Or you need to develop good friends who you care for and who care or you!

In those areas, I have been very lucky.

Of course, my son has been the center of my life and will always be the center of my love. When he was young, I was the rock in his life. Now that I am old, he is the rock in my life.

Selected Thoughts on Politics & Social Life

The following are excerpted from letters to my son:

- When you return to Antigua again, you will not be landing at Coolidge International Airport. That has been washed into the sea. You will be landing at V.C. Bird International Airport. So don't be surprised. Political tidal wave washed away Coolidge. October 31, 1985.

- Cricket is being played here and it is causing a lot of problems. Bird allowed some English people who played cricket in South Africa to play here today. Most of the people here don't seem to like it and they didn't have much people attend on the first day. However, some liberation fellows here, got some posters and were sticking them up around the Recreation Grounds. Police saw them and locked two of them up. Their parents paid $500 each to bail them out. One of the head of the Liberation group went to the police station to see them and they locked him up too. Aubrey (Webson), then went, and they wanted to lock him up too. But what saved him is that he is blind! Politics is a corrupt business. Why do they want to lock up people for protesting? Black politicians lock up black protestors for protesting against white cricketers who supported White racist South Africa! Imagine that! Bird should be ashamed of himself… he should never mention a word about his efforts with Moody Stuart again. Never! February 9th, 1986.

- All of life in Antigua is based on politics or religion. I guess all of life in most places is based on politics or religion. Politicians try to divide people into one party or another. We are even divided and fighting based on race, or country, or the color of your skin. Religions divide you into one thing or another: Christian, Muslim, Jew or Hindu – or something else. Even the Christians divide their own: Seventh Day, Baptist, Catholic, Anglican… But their Bible says that we must multiply… not divide! September 19th, 1986.

- Hector and Lester always fighting… like two people in love… I wouldn't be surprised if they aren't secret friends. June 24, 1987.

- I just read in the newspaper about that airport money situation. There was no mention of Reuben (Harris) in it… but everybody says that he wanted the resignation of Vere Junior because he (Reuben) says that Vere is a thief. The same French people are lending Bird more money: $15 million to finish fixing the airport! Antilles (radio station) says that that is a lie and Papa Bird said that he is sorry to know that Antilles has said such a thing. $15 million! I wonder how much they going take from that to line their pockets? Aug 29, 1987.

- Papa Bird says that he is building up Antigua… by putting mud in front of our house (at Perry Bay). Soon Antigua is going to be 120 square miles – just from the mud that they are putting around the place! April 27th, 1988.

- 'Hadeed and dem' grapping up every spot of land in Antigua. They seem to have Bird wrapped around them finger. Soon from now when you want a piece of land to buy, you may have to go to Barbuda. And… I hear that all they have over there is sand! Lester and them going after that soon too! May 26th 1988.

- The UNDP folks passed around here last evening: Lionel (Gomes – our neighbor), Baldwin Spencer and two others. I told them my mind. They only know people when they want to get in power, after that they give you a kick in your rear end and leave you right there. They tried to defend themselves. Spencer said you are his friend and that he sometimes writes you. You never told me that! Anything go so? June 17th, 1988.

- We have some new neighbors. They are light skinned. They don't talk a word of English. Only Spanish. Someone said that they didn't come from Joey's, or the place called Skells, or that place in Hatton, or the place with the stupid name 'Home away from home.' We have all kinds of people coming to Antigua… Bird and them let everybody through the gates… front gate, side gate and back gate. Well… I came through the gate too… long time ago so I guess I can't complain. But soon from now… most of the people in Grays Farm are going to be from somewhere else… Dominica, Montserrat, Santo Domingo, Guyana… and who knows where else. August 22, 1988.

- Somebody just brought me a calendar with D.C. Christian's picture on it. Its election time… so he show up – on a calendar. It says "Honest, Decent & Humble". It should say one word – "Absent". January 9th, 1989.

- Tim Hector was in the 'pasture' on Saturday saying his recitation. He had his motorcade yesterday. February 6, 1989.

- Selling cocaine is the new thing in Antigua. Cocaine is getting plentiful like bread… When it's not cocaine – it's clothes or chicken or something… Every Tom, Dick and Harry is on the street selling clothes. They go to St. Martin and Puerto Rico to shop… but people are saying that the Coke that they peddle on the side in secret is what put them on their feet in public. I know a woman who just bought a new fridge and washing machine. She says that the money come from the "box money she throw." Other people say that she push Coke. That's the new lifestyle around here. And now you don't know who is who and who is doing what. March 27th 1989.

- Papa and Lester's road that they are building from the bottom of Donavans to the 'backwall' where the fishing boats dock, is 'coming to come'. They think that this "Red Sea Road" will save them from the people of Greenbay and Grays Farm. Because the Birds hate us so much, what they (are) really doing is trying to bypass Grays Farm and Greenbay by building a road in the sea. They don't want the tourists to pass through Grays Farm and see how they have turned their backs on us. Their time will come. June 3, 1989.

- Everything here is quiet on the outside, but on the inside, I think that the Birdies pots are boiling over. They have as much meetings as if election is near. They are trying to cover up their 'night soil'. The radio said this morning that Cochrane shouted at a Birdie meeting last night that anything the Premier says or does he back it up 100%. That's life. What else do you expect? October 9, 1989.

- Don't ever get involved in politics! It is a dirty game. You get pressured and then get high blood pressure, nerve trouble, ulcerated stomach… you name it.

Instead, look for peace and quiet where you can relax. October 9, 1989.

- Today Labor is back in power – again. But, D.C. Christian lost. Baldwin Spencer won and he is the only opposition candidate that win his seat – plus the Barbuda candidate who I think was independent. Not sure how this 'one one' situation will help Greenbay or Barbuda!

- Antiguans are a 'beggie beggie people'. That's why 'Bird and them' could stay in power so long. People beg them for jobs… and beg them for everything else. And of course Bird and his chosen few could get everything they want from people in return for the few handouts that they give people. In the 1960's and 70's Bird and them used to hand out food… dry milk and sugar and flour… People used to line up to get their supplies. Of course, Bird used the 'beggie beggie' mentality to grab their vote (and some of them even give their daughters.) I think he ended up grabbing more than their vote… he grabbed and put a lasso around them head (minds) also. Even now… all those old people and even their children and grand-children still won't let go of

Bird… all because when they begged – he gave them the crumbs from the table… while he and his kept the lion share for themselves. He sent his sons to college… to study law… while he kept Antigua and Barbuda people begging for flour, sugar and dry milk. October 12, 1991.

- I listen to the 'voice of the people' and while some of the voices preach wisdom – most of the voices show a high level of 'tupidenss' and ignorance. While it is good that everyone can 'have their say', a lot of what they have to say is foolishness. I guess it's as a result of the modern age for my ears to be assaulted by the 'tupidness' everyday. At least I am alive to hear people make a fool of themselves. I guess also that according to (The Mighty) Bold Face (calypsonian) 'If them no know… them just no know.'

- It is because of ignorance why most of us are still in slavery and bondage to slick sick politicians. Our ignorance allows them to control us.

On Parenting

On Parenting

Parenting is very important. It is probably the most important task of adults. The way we do our jobs determines the quality and character of the next generation... and the next and the next... This of course depends on if our children and their children carry on the teachings and values and morals that they learn from us.

As I look around what I see is that parents are too busy with their own lives to pay very close attention to what children are learning and doing. Because these parents are busy, they spend a lot of time shouting at their kids rather than teaching them. I may be wrong with this... because they are teaching them... but it probably is not what they parents think that they are passing on.

I have always believed that telling children what to do is not as good as showing them what to do. Showing them is more powerful.

Some parents teach one thing with their mouths and teach another with their activities and behaviors. So what are children learning? I am no psychologist... but I strongly believe that children pay more attention to what we do… rather than what we say.

I believe that it is our behaviors and activities that we are passing on to children – not our preachings or teachings.

I have tried to teach my son a set of values and morals to guide him. I have lived my life in a certain way to 'show him how'. I hope that he is passing these on to his sons. I have tried to live my life in a way that my son can see how adults should live. I have encouraged him to teach himself about life. I encouraged him to be involved in as many activities as possible while he was growing up. I didn't have money but I had ideas… and so what I could not give him in material things, I tried to give him in knowledge, believing, doing and thinking.

I encouraged him to be in sports and so he played cricket and soccer… and even though he was somewhat overweight… he tried his hand at athletics. He got involved in martial arts and also was involved in weight-lifting or body building during his years in Secondary School.

All of this kept him out of trouble. And I think he learned self-discipline. One of the things that I am glad for is that his involvement in all of these activities kept him distant from the neighborhood kids. He grew up in Grays Farm and Greenbay. It is not because all the neighborhood kids were bad… but they did not show the kinds of morals that I was teaching my son. Apparently, their parents were not teaching them what I was teaching him. So, he grew up as a kind of loner… But I don't think he was lonely. He was always reading something… comics, story books and even as a small child… very advance books on metaphysics and metapsychology.

Those were my books… and books that my father had given me. My son had read them all by the time he was twelve.

So he was busy reading, exercising, learning and growing his knowledge as he grew up.

Another thing that I think is important is that we should be totally responsible for our children's upbringing. When my son was between the ages of five and eight, I did a lot of traveling throughout the countryside selling all kinds of trinkets etc. Every Sunday I traveled to the St. Pauls area or St. Mary's. I never ever left my son with anyone. He trudged right along by my side. Every Sunday. I decided that was not going to leave him with the neighbors or anyone else. He was my responsibility. Everything I did involved him. And he knew it.

That was a feature of my whole life. This was my son... my responsibility. If he was to grow up in the kind of son that I wanted... then that was my responsibility... until he was responsible for himself. And that included his teenage years.

You see I am a firm believer that we are parents for life. No matter what my age is... or what his age is... he is still my son! Yes... long ago he became responsible for his own life. But I have always been here to help... to advise and sometimes to critique. I have always been – and at 97... I still am available to advise! And I do!

Today, many parents don't seem to have the zest to push their kids into the areas that they know they should go. Children must be pushed where they don't want to go. The ideas that you are going to make your nine or ten year old child decide what he/she wants to do, how he/she wants to do it... is ridiculous... at least to me.

We decide where we want to push them and then force them by whatever means necessary to get them to do it. When they get to young adults... they can choose whether they want to continue or not. However, they will now have a background... a basis on which to make their life decisions.

It is a mistake to wait until they are teenagers to get them involved in activities. By then it is too late. Some adults complain that we must let children be children and allow them to run around and play. However, based on what I am seeing on the TV news, while our children are playing on the computers and watching TV, children in Japan and other countries are learning to build those same computers and television. Our children are growing up behind. By the time they get to the teenage years, they are woefully behind other children in other parts of the world.

Home is the Training School for Abroad

I learned from my father and from the adults that I grew up around that "home is the training school for abroad." What this means is that children should be taught at home everything that they need in the outside world. When you get well trained at home… you are prepared to be effective when you go anywhere else. The right attitudes, moral character and skills in life start in the home.

So home training involves children learning about managing their time, organizing their room, planning their day to day activities, respecting adults, contributing to the household chores, cleaning up after themselves, and generally taking responsibility for their own life and success. If they don't learn these things at home... where else and when else will they learn them? And, who will teach them?

One problem is that many parents did not themselves get these trainings... so if they have not learned them... they can't pass them on.

The other things is that some parents don't seem to know how to talk and relate to their children. Instead of talking in a caring manner, they shout and carry on. They threaten. They use indecent language. They talk to their children in the same manner that they talk to other adults. And of course as a result, they turn off their children's zest for life... They give their children a false sense of how you discipline while loving and of how you show care while correcting. I am sure that my son will tell you that I have never shouted at him... I have never threatened him... As a matter of fact... I don't remember ever hitting him. He knew what I expected and he did just that. He knew that I would be disappointed if he misbehaved... so he didn't. I know he didn't want to disappoint me... even if he was tempted. So... it is all in the way we relate to our children and the connection that we have with them.

Many parents need training themselves. I think that this has become a worldwide necessity. But… and this is important… we must be careful of who we get to train parents! Are they training their kids according to the ideas (principles) that they are sharing with other parents?

One of the blockages and hindrances to parent training kids of things (activities) is that some parents don't want other adults to tell them anything about how to raise their kids. We must try to overcome this since many parents (and their children) need help.

The other group of people who need training on how to work with kids are teachers. A lot of them might be knowledgeable about whatever it is they are teaching… but they know nothing about how to connect and correct children. They too resort to shouting, threatening, demanding and being arrogant with the children in their care. As a young girl, my first job was teaching. I remember that in teacher training we learned how to teach math and English. But we also learned about teaching 'etiquette'.

Let's push our children and grandchildren. Let's set good examples as parents. Let's not only preach and teach… let's show by our behaviors and activities.

Thoughts on Faith & Wisdom

Hard Work

Don't shy away from hard work. "By the sweat of thy brow shalt thou live."

The work that most people do these days don't make them sweat... at least not from 'hard' or physical work. So, I think that 'hard work' these days is supposed to be important, challenging, or difficult work.

'Hard work' also means that you have to work steadily, without shying away from giving everything that you have got and without shirking from your duty, your obligation or your commitment. And even though you sit at a desk... you may still sweat from the challenges, risks, or just from the importance of what you are doing.

Sometimes, as I sit on my gallery and watch the planes fly pass on their way to landing at the airport, I often wonder about the stress that those pilots experience – particularly flying at night and in bad weather.

Another type of 'hard work' these days is 'teaching' those kids who bring drugs and weapons to school, while others want to beat up their teachers. For the serious and responsible teacher having to deal with those children — that's hard work.

Teaching

Teaching is probably the best profession. As I said before, I used to be a teacher when I was young. Teaching in my day was different than what it is today. These days… for many teachers… teaching is just another job. A lot of them don't put in the effort to teach kids. As a matter of thinking, teaching is not a job… it is more like a calling. You are responsible for moulding young children into adults.

Teaching is a profession where you treat each child as you would treat your own – you teach them with their best interest in mind.

As a teacher, if your children aren't doing well as students that means that you are not doing well as a teacher. You can't blame children when they fail… because a lot of times it is you who have failed them. You are the one with a failing grade.

Teaching doesn't take place just in the classroom. It takes place in the community and in the village. That is why many of the old 'long ago' teachers were respected by everybody. They were addressed respectfully by all as

"Teacher Jennifer" or "Teacher Georgette", etc.

Most teachers today want the respect from the community and parents – before they have proved that they have earned it. They think that just because they have a job as a teacher… that the respect comes with the job. No. The respect is earned. And it is earned the hard way… in the classroom and in the community.

What have you done beyond what you are paid to do? Who have you helped outside of the normal hours of teaching? And how many have you helped? And have you used your own time and money and other things to help your students and their parents?

Avoid Business Partnerships

According to my father, a partnership is a 'leaky ship'. Stay away from business partnerships. If you have to be involved in one, keep your eyes on the money and the goods or your partner may 'steal you blind.' People are always looking out for themselves. In a partnership… it usually starts with lots of promises and nice talk about commitment and 'fifty-fifty' etc. But when the need for hard work shows up – that is when your partner goes missing. He forgets about sharing 'fifty-fifty' in the work. But when the money shows up – your partner is there to take the credit and demand his part of the 'fifty-fifty' the profit.

Control Your Own Thoughts

One of the most important recommendations from me is that you control what goes on in your mind. You may not be able to control your surroundings or your environment. You certainly cannot control other people. But you can control what goes on in your own head. You can control your own thinking. And you must be focused on this every second, every minute, every day. So as you read this, what are you thinking right now? What are your thoughts?

Controlling what goes on in your head is not easy. Most times, it seems as if your thoughts are controlling you. I try to do this through prayer. I pray often. And I do so in the peace and quiet of my own head. No one knows that I am praying. They may see me being quiet… but they don't really know what's going on inside. I keep this private because this is my personal vault… no one needs to know what's in it or what is working on or processing. That's my business – not theirs. (I don't know how… but my son has figured how when I am praying!)

In controlling my own thoughts, I don't allow what other people think or say influence me or my attitude. I don't allow what I hear on the news to change my thinking. I don't allow what my neighbors say to control my own beliefs. I don't allow what the politicians say to change what I think. I don't allow what the experts say to determine what I think. And, most importantly, I don't allow what the so-called spiritual leaders (priests, parsons, reverends, bishops, popes…) to influence my own thoughts… or my actions.

I certainly listen to them. I read what they said. And then I compare it with my own deep, inner beliefs. I check to see whether or not what they say looks right, sounds right or feels.

So for example, when a spiritual leader, who is voted in to 'religious political power by others' is claimed to be 'infallible' – I put that in the corner of my mind where such claims belong!

Read widely… Read deeply… Read for understanding… and when you read don't believe blindly.

To my son: Control your own thoughts and keep the most powerful ones private. Reveal them only to your sons…

and do that carefully… and only when they are ready to receive.

The Power of Belief

On the subject of belief... please check your beliefs and explore where they came from.

Don't believe your own beliefs blindly.

Sometimes your beliefs come from people who have influenced you. Their beliefs came from someone who influenced them. And their beliefs came from some book they read, some story that made an impression on them... something they made up... or something like that.

Your beliefs are sometimes hidden in history and mystery. But because they are in your head or in your gut... you grab hold of them and accept them blindly because you think "these are my beliefs." The truth of the matter is that you really don't know the origin of some of them. You probably picked them up along the way like a virus entering your mind. Some you grabbed consciously and some sneaked into your mental home and stayed there... growing... growing... sticking... sticking... until they called your brain – their home.

So be careful of believing your own beliefs. And be even more careful of grabbing on to other people's beliefs. Why? Because they got their beliefs the same way. And many people are so hooked into their beliefs that they are willing to kill others or to die for them. And a lot of the beliefs that they are willing to die for – in my mind – are stupid beliefs.

As a matter of fact… many people are willing to die for other people's beliefs! Like young poor people going to war to protect rich people's, philosophy, interests, properties and ways of life. These young people die so that rich politicians and bankers and legal thieves can continue to con the rest of the world. Or they die for communism or the American 'isms (capitalism)… or whatever the 'ism of the day or the place is. Teenagers (who go to war) have been conned in dying for something they really know nothing about. They are really dying for other people's beliefs.

I have told my son that he should teach his sons to develop their own beliefs and to constantly examine (evaluate) where these beliefs came from and how they developed and if they still make sense (to them).

The bottom line is that my grandsons and other young people must develop beliefs that are life sustaining and constantly protect their thoughts and beliefs from the influence of others.

Your brain is the bank that every thief (politician, priest, business person) wants to break into and control. Once they have control of your brain and your beliefs… they own you. And they own you while you strongly believe that you are in control of you.

It is the most powerful source of control in the world. The best examples of this are in politics, religion and business (marketing)!

On the other hand, when you believe something that you have figured out in the space of your own brain, hold on to it and guard it carefully. When I say figured out, I mean that you have carefully thought about it, looked at it from seven angles, unwrapped it, peeling it like a banana or like an onion… and continue to do so… daily adding and subtracting… fitting new things into it… and taking away those things that don't make any sense anymore.

Believe in Yourself – Not in What People Say

Don't believe the 'authorities', 'experts', 'professionals' or 'specialists'. Their knowledge of the world is linked to the current limits of information. Throughout my 97 years, I have seen so much change that it is dizzying. 'Experts' come and they go. Today – they site one thing as an absolute truth and then tomorrow they cite something else as the 'new absolute truth.'

When you read the books on science – whether they are about medicine or economics… you realize that truth in scientific things is fleeting… The first writing(edition) of any book is always totally different from the later writing (edition)… And sometimes, new 'scientific' 'evidence' totally proves old scientific 'truths' and 'facts' to be wrong.

So we need to be skeptical of anyone… scientist or politician – priest or police – who preach or teach about 'facts'.

I have learned to keep my own counsel. I have learned to listen to the thoughts of others without being swayed to accept 'truth' or 'falsehood'.

As a matter of fact, I have adopted the practice of looking at everything, every fact, and so-called evidence with skepticism. Why? Because I understand that things change – and sometimes they change radically… and very very quickly.

Live Life to the Fullest

Live your life to the fullest on Earth. Make your Heaven here on Earth. Get the best life possible right here. Don't dream of going somewhere else when you are dead. This Heaven... the one right here is certain. Live it powerfully. Live it spiritually. Live it prayerfully. Take it from someone who is 97 years of age. I think that focusing on living a beautiful life after you are dead is a waste of precious time while you are alive. (Now that I am 97 – I can afford to focus on what's next...)

Endeavor to live life fully and in abundance. Build your Heaven here on Earth. Rather than waiting to die so that we can travel to Heaven... we should focus our lives on building Heaven right here! World and village peace, prosperity, abundance, personal satisfaction, health, personal freedom, an environment that nourishes, long and productive life, sense of community and supportive family are all aspects of Heaven on Earth.

So... I believe that Heaven is right here on Earth. If you live your life here by following those principles that you think will get you into some distant Heaven, you will reap the rewards right now… right here on Earth. And maybe later… you will reap it there too!

Other Thoughts and Perspectives

- As I get older, I have a lot of pain here and there… but my pain is a message for me to celebrate that I am still alive… and that I can't take that for granted. The younger we are – the more we seem to take life for granted… we act as if it will always be there… we don't treat it like in the extra-special and extra-careful way that we should treat our most important asset.

  Life is all that we have here on Earth. And since they say that tomorrow is not promised… we should live today fully. I wouldn't say live it as if it is our last… some people might take that to mean that they should go out and do something stupid. No… what I mean is that we should live it by doing all the positive and uplifting things that make us feel spiritually powerful, healthy and happy.

Don't put aside anything to do tomorrow. Do it today. Do it now.

- They say that the wells of providence are deep, but it is the bucket we take to it that is small. So we either have to make our bucket bigger, carry more buckets or take plenty trips. I have done all of those. When other people were sleeping I was carrying buckets to the well of providence using prayer as vehicle.

- Watch your mind carefully. It will create your Heaven or your hell.

- Whatever you do… always prepare to win… prepare for success. Don't spend any time preparing for failure. If negative things happen you are already prepared to turn them into success.

- The world does not pay for what a person knows. It pays for what a person does with what she knows. I understood this when I started my own business helping people. People came to me for help because they thought I had the knowledge and that I 'could do things' for them. When they came, I was ready. I had spent my life reading and learning at my father's feet.

- I love the idea that every day we must "water the root to enjoy the fruit." The way I understand that is that we must pay attention to the root of life to enjoy the fruits of life. You don't even water the root… you water the soil… the roots are nourished and provide you with your reward – the fruit!

- I try to have a certain type of atmosphere around me that will show peace and kindness from the inside to the outside.

- If you fear something you will attract it in your life. If you hate someone you will keep attracting that kind of person in your life -over and over and over. Conquer your fear, hate and other negative feelings. You must love that which you fear... Love the person you hate... and your love will zero-them-out (neutralize) them into non-existence and non-importance.

- We are not millionaires but 'pennyaires'. The thing is that pennies become millions if you gather and keep enough of them.

- There is peace on earth for him (and her) who sends good thoughts, blessings and 'goodwill to others' all during the year!

- Marcus, I am taking it easy, praying and meditating. I have confidence that God will make a way for you, he will work things out. Just trust him.

- Worry and hurry are two things to avoid. Both of them will kill you. You worry about something that hasn't happened yet and most of the time your worry never comes true anyway. You wasted all that time and energy for nothing. Worry is in your mind. Hurry is also in your mind. You are hurrying because of how you think. If you have to hurry or if you have a hurry attitude it means that you don't prepare well. You are not using your time well. For a lot of people hurry is a habit… and it's a bad habit.

- Education is great and it is very important. But according to Mr. Brown… "studyation beats education". Whatever business you are in you have to study it – find out what the books don't tell you. Find out what those who are successful will never reveal. Uncover your own 'secrets' to success. Yes… education is great… you can learn a lot… But remember that its role is to set you on the path of getting your own knowledge.

- It is OK to have abundance... wealth and prosperity... money and property... but you must be careful how you get those. How you get something is more important than what you get. The 'how' may come back to haunt you – or yours!

- If you follow the best principles of life you will never have to regret your life. If you follow the laws of nature... nature will reward you.

- I have never seen a house built with rotten wood... but we are trying to build a nation with rotten politicians. And if they didn't come in rotten... they end up rotten!

- I think that people should always tell the truth even under difficult circumstances. Telling the truth means honesty and openness in all of our relating with others. I believe that when we withhold the truth we put a lot of pressure on ourselves. We hold back what we really believe... we hold back on how we really feel... and we hold back from being true to ourselves.

- Follow the laws of the world… the laws of nature and you will do well.

What Lies Ahead?

What Lies Ahead?

At this age of 97, I have a lot of questions about what lies ahead. Something is wrong with the current story that people die and go to hell or Heaven. First of all, everyone should be going to Heaven, since the preachers say that "Jesus died for our sins."

If he died for our sins… we shouldn't have to die… and if we die we should all be going to Heaven. I still don't understand that message.

With regards to hell and Heaven… those two things don't make much sense to me… Where is Heaven and where is hell? On another planet? Which planet? When I was young, the preachers used to tell us that the River Jordan was in Heaven and therefore if we were good, we would cross Jordan and get through the gates into Heaven.

I was shocked to find out that Jordan was a place on the map… a real place… and that neither crossing the River Jordan or the River Euphrates would get you into the place called Heaven. So what does this do the idea of Heaven that all of us have accepted… and continue to accept?

Those stories just don't make any sense, but they have all of us believing it. Not only that… people are afraid to challenge those stories which, when you really think of them… they don't seem to have any basis at all.

So, I have a lot of questions, not only about Heaven and hell and their location… and even whether such places really exist.

The people who are confident about Heaven and hell… have never been there. And when I ask 'so-called' religious people about the location of Heaven… they tell me that the location is not important (that's because they don't know where it is).

The only people who know about Heaven and hell are dead… And none of them have ever come back to tell us the truth. So, the living don't know… and the dead won't or can't tell us! And to complicate matters, the Catholic church tell us that there is a place in between: purgatory!

So is there life after death?

I have promised my son one thing. When I die, I will find out. And I promise that I will come back and tell him! And neither God, the Devil or their angels will be able to stop me!

I must say another thing to my son: Make your Heaven here on earth. Live to live. Teach that to your sons… Do good and do well. That's what they should learn. Look out for their families. Look out for their friends. Look out for their community. But… look out for themselves first… so that they can help others. Live good… and live well.

And, live right. Righteous means living life in the right way. Don't break man's laws… and don't break any spiritual laws. Use common sense. Do good to others as you would have them do to you. And when you can't do good… do nothing!

Yes… what's next is on my mind a lot because I want to know where I am going. Or is this it? Is this all there is?

If this is all there is to life… just living on Earth – working… working… working… and more working just so that you can keep a roof over your head and food in your belly… and working for your family… If that is all there is then it is a lot… But for me it is not enough… I am expecting more.

But, if this is all there is to life… then we are no better than the birds and the bees… living just to live.

On the other hand, if this is all there is to life... people should live it fully and live it right.

So, I have come to the conclusion that there is no certainty about what's next. I guess that's why the various religions hype up that mysterious place called 'Heaven' as the place that's next.

Again, I am not sure why they talk so much about hell (sometimes in the same sentence)... unless it is a scare thing they use to get you to come to church to fill their collection plates.

But talking up and making a big thing about Heaven works for poor people who don't have anything else to look forward to.

Yes the rich go to church too... but they have tons of money to use for their expensive toys. But poor people, who feel 'down' everyday... who have to scratch like yard fowl for their livelihood... don't have anything to look forward to... other than more scratching tomorrow, next week and next year... and the year after that.

So here comes the preacher talking about going to Heaven... living with the angels... no need for food or drink – and of course – no need for any day to day scratching up there.

So, the story about Heaven, works well among poor people. It also works for rich and powerful people too. In order to clear their conscience from getting rich off of the backs of poor people, they piously go to church on Sunday… put some money in the pray (pay) basket, and return on Monday to rob and/or separate people from of their hard earned pennies. Then they go to confession on Friday (I am not too sure they still do that) and get forgiveness from the priest so that they can do some more the next week. It is one merry-go-round.

So, the story about Heaven works for everybody.

Of course, they say you have to have faith. The faith that they are talking about is faith in their version of scripture… and their interpretation of what Heaven is.

I do have faith. Plenty of it. As a matter of fact, my whole life has been based on faith and prayer and spiritual practices. But I don't agree with the version of Heaven and hell that the uninformed religious 'experts' give every Sunday. I don't agree with their version of the kind of faith that they speak about and that they ensure is that we must have.

I have faith in God. I have faith in a God who is universal and who responds to my prayers. I have faith in a God who is personal for me... and I don't need anyone else to go between God and me.

I can go directly to my God. And... who knows, God is probably a woman and not the warlike male figure that people have painted. My God is peaceful, forgiving, loving, caring and looks out for everyone. My God doesn't pick favorites. My God doesn't choose between one political party or the other. My God is universal for: Muslim and Jews, Catholic and Protestant, Adventist and Baptist, Hindu and all the rest... for everyone.

Whatever is next for me... I look forward to with openness and with a clean and clear heart.

In my heart, I feel that this is not it! I feel that there is a next chapter... one that I can look forward to with excitement, and one that I can and do embrace fully.

I am at peace with my past.

I am open to my future... whatever and wherever the new journey may take me.

On the other hand, I am really looking forward to what I have control over at this moment. I am here right now… looking forward to writing my next book!

I am also looking forward to hearing from you! Please email me at: HyacinthMottley@gmail.com or contact my son Dr. Marcus Mottley at: mpowerme@gmail.com .

Made in the USA
Coppell, TX
29 September 2020